States United

Rifles and Riflemen at the Battle of Kings Mountain

History No. 12

States United

Rifles and Riflemen at the Battle of Kings Mountain
History No. 12

ISBN/EAN: 9783337626648

Printed in Europe, USA, Canada, Australia, Japan

Cover: Foto ©ninafisch / pixelio.de

More available books at **www.hansebooks.com**

NATIONAL PARK SERVICE
POPULAR STUDY SERIES

History No. 12

Rifles and Riflemen
at the
Battle of Kings Mountain

UNITED STATES DEPARTMENT OF THE
INTERIOR, J. A. KRUG, Secretary

NATIONAL PARK SERVICE, NEWTON B. DRURY, Director

Reprinted 1947

CONTENTS

For sale by the Superintendent of Documents, U. S. Government
Printing Office, Washington 25, D. C.—Price 15 cents

*Maj. Patrick Ferguson, British commander at the Battle of Kings Mountain,
and inventor of the breechloading rifle bearing his name; from a marble
bust.*

Kings Mountain

A Hunting Rifle Victory [1]

By Roger W. Young, Historian
Branch of History

Kings Mountain, the fierce attack of American frontiersmen on October 7, 1780, against Cornwallis' scouting force under Ferguson, was an unexpected onslaught carried out in the foothills of South Carolina. This sudden uprising of the stalwart Alleghany mountaineers, for the protection of their homes and people from the threat of Tory invasion under British leadership, was relatively isolated in conception and execution from the main course of the Revolutionary War in the South.

Clearly uncontemplated in the grand British design to subjugate the South in a final effort to end the Revolution, this accidental encounter in the Southern Piedmont delayed incidentally, but did not alter materially, the movement of Britain's Southern Campaign. Kings Mountain is notable chiefly perhaps as supplying the first definite forewarning of the impending British military disasters of 1781. It was decisive to the extent that it contributed the earliest distinct element of defeat to the final major British campaign of the Revolution.

The extraordinary action occurred during one of the bleakest periods of the Revolution. A major change in British military strategy had again shifted the scene of action to the South in 1778. Faced by a discouraging campaign in the North and assuming that the reputed

Loyalist sympathies of the South would be more conducive to a victory there, the British war ministry had dictated the immediate subjugation of the South. With the conquered Southern provinces as a base of operations, the war office planned to crush Washington's armies in the North and East between offensives from North and South, and thus bring the defeat of the more stubborn Revolutionary Northern colonies.

Unimpeded by effective resistance, this Southern Campaign swept unchecked through Georgia and part of South Carolina during 1778-79. The surrender of Gen. Benjamin Lincoln's American army at Charleston, in May 1780, greatly strengthened the British hold on South Carolina. Encouraged by the British successes, the Royalist and Tory elements of the Georgia and South Carolina lowlands rose in increasingly large numbers to the support of the Royal cause. Soon most of South Carolina, except a few districts in the Piedmont, were overrun by British and Royalist forces directed by Cornwallis, and he was maturing plans for the invasion of North Carolina. His designs were upset temporarily by the advance of a new American Army under Gates. Meeting Cornwallis near Camden, August 16, 1780, Gates suffered a disastrous defeat, again leaving South Carolina and the route northward open to the British. By September, Cornwallis again had undertaken the invasion of North Carolina, gaining a foothold at Charlotte, a center of Whig power, after a skirmish there late that month.

The sole Southern region in the path of Cornwallis' northward march which had remained undisturbed by the course of the war lay in the foothills and ranges of the Alleghanies stretching through northwestern South Carolina, western North Carolina, and into the present eastern Tennessee. Only here, among the frontier settlements of the independent mountain yeoman, could the patriotic Whigs find refuge, late in the summer of 1780, from their despised enemies, the propertied Royalist and Tory forces aroused by Cornwallis. Occupied with establishing a new frontier and protecting their rude homes from the nearer threat of the border Indians, the mountain men had been little concerned with the war on the seaboard. The influx of partisan Whig forces seeking sanctuary first brought the effects of war vividly before them. But from the free and comparatively peaceful existence, the backwoodsmen were soon to be aroused to the protection of their homes and possessions by a threat of direct aggression.

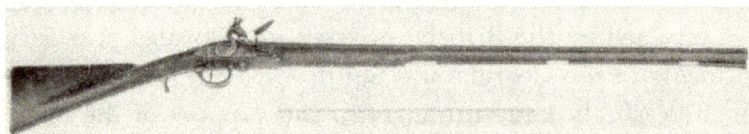

Only a few of the original Ferguson rifles are extant. The one shown is exhibited at Kings Mountain National Military Park, South Carolina. Here we see the profile of the piece with an 18-inch ruler to indicate scale.

That threat came from Maj. Patrick Ferguson, of Cornwallis' command, who, after Camden, had been ordered to operate in the South Carolina Piedmont to suppress the Whig opposition remaining there and to arouse the back country Tories, organizing their strength in support of the British cause. Encountering little organized Whig resistance, and having rapidly perfected the Tory strength in the Piedmont, Ferguson in September 1780 undertook a foray against Gilbert Town, a Whig outpost in North Carolina, near the present town of Rutherfordton. Fearful of such an invasion, the border leaders, Isaac Shelby, of Sullivan County, and John Sevier, of Washington County, North Carolina (both now in Tennessee), had hurried to the Watauga settlements and called for volunteers to defeat Ferguson. They also forwarded urgent appeals for aid to Wilkes, Surry, Burke, and Rutherford Counties in North Carolina, and to Washington County in Virginia.

From Gilbert Town, early in September, Ferguson dispatched his famed invidious threat over the mountains to the backwoodsmen, warning them "that if they did not desist from their opposition to the British arms and take protection under his standard, he would march his army over the mountains, hang their leaders, and lay their country waste with fire and sword." Actually this was but an empty gesture from Ferguson who was then preparing one final foray across the border in South Carolina before making a junction with Cornwallis at Charlotte. Yet, to the freedom-loving frontier leaders the threat became a challenge which strengthened their determination to destroy the invader. Thus spurred, they assembled quickly, each in hunting garb, with knapsack, blanket, and long hunting rifle, most of them mounted, but some afoot. They were united by a strong resolve to destroy Ferguson and his Tory force, even though they had many a brother, cousin, or even a father among the back country men in his command. In fact, the partisan and internecine warfare, which raged during the Revolution through the southern highlands and along the Piedmont with members of the same family arrayed against each other as Whig and Tory, reached a climax in the Kings Mountain expedition and engagement.

Assembling near the present Elizabethton, Tenn., late in September, the mountaineers circled southeastward into upper South Carolina, in swift pursuit of Ferguson. Joining the forces of Shelby and Sevier were the Virginians under Campbell, and as the expedition marched southward it was augmented by the border fighters under McDowell and Cleveland. Though characterized by daring impulse, the purpose of this strategic frontier uprising had been conceived coolly by these leaders, and its execution, in pursuit and assault, was to be brilliantly carried out. At the Cowpens in upper South Carolina, the expedition was joined October 6 by further volunteers under local Whig leaders, including Chronicle, Williams, Lacey, and Hawthorne. Recruits brought definite word of Ferguson's whereabouts near Kings Mountain. And there, in a final council of war, were selected 910 stalwart fighting men, all mounted, who immediately moved through the night upon the position of Ferguson's Provincial Corps and Tory militia, now encamped atop the Kings Mountain spur.

Despite the added discomfort to their already fatigued bodies and mounts, the expedition pushed determinedly through the cold night rain, and en route the leaders, now commanded by Campbell, devised a final plan of attack. Having agreed to surround the spur and gradually to close in upon its defenders from all sides, the Whig attackers engaged the 1,104 British Provincials, Tories, and Loyalists at about 3 o'clock on the afternoon of October 7, 1780. In the sanguinary one-hour engagement that ensued along the heavily wooded and rocky slopes, the backwoodsmen, veterans of countless border clashes even if untrained in formal warfare, gained a complete victory, killing or capturing the entire British force. The most illustrious casualty was, of course, Maj. Patrick Ferguson, the British commander.

The extraordinary action is memorable primarily as an example of the personal valor and resourcefulness of the American frontier fighter, particularly the Scotch-Irish, during the Revolution. It demonstrated the proficiency with which he took advantage of natural cover and capitalized upon the ineffectiveness of the British downhill angle of fire in successfully assaulting Ferguson's position. The resulting casualties clearly exhibited the unerring accuracy of the long rifle used in skilled hands, even when confronted with the menace of Ferguson's bayonet charges. The engagement also afforded one of the most interesting demonstrations during the Revolution of the use of the novel breechloading Ferguson rifle. The Kings Mountain expedition and engagement illustrated the characteristic vigor of the untrained American frontiersman in rising to the threat of border invasion. It recorded his military effectiveness in overcoming such a danger and his initiative in disbanding quietly upon its passing, especially when guided by strategy and tactics momentarily devised by partisan leaders of the caliber of Shelby, Sevier, Campbell, Cleveland, and Lacey.

To the long standing local strife between Whig and Tory, the results of Kings Mountain were direct and considerable. It was an unexpected blow which completely unnerved and undermined the Loyalist organization in the Carolinas, and placed the downtrodden Whig cause of the Piedmont in the ascendancy. Kings Mountain was a climax to the social, economic, and military clashes between democratic Whig and propertied Tory elements. In a sense it epitomized this bitter struggle and its abrupt ending on what then was the southwestern frontier. Heartening to the long repressed Whigs, the engagement placed them in the control of the Piedmont, and encouraged them to renewed resistance.

The disintegration of Loyalist power in the Carolinas after Kings Mountain temporarily proved a real obstacle to Cornwallis' hitherto unchecked northward movement. The demoralization of the Loyalist forces, which were the main reliance for local support in the prosecution of his campaign, left Cornwallis precariously situated in hostile North Carolina territory with a renewed Whig threat to the rear in South Carolina. Momentarily discouraged, he halted his North Carolina offensive and retired from his foothold at Charlotte to a defensive position at Winnsboro, in upper South Carolina. Here he remained inactive, with his campaign at a standstill, until the approach of reinforcements at his rear, under Leslie, enabled him to resume his invasion of North Carolina early in January 1781.

This time Cornwallis' march was more cautious in its initial stages. For the enforced delay of the major British advance occasioned by Kings Mountain and lengthened by indecision, had enabled Greene, the new American commander in the South, to reorganize his shattered and dispirited army and launch a renewed and two-fold offensive upon the main British movement. It was this offensive in 1781, which first successfully struck the British at Cowpens, then rapidly withdrew through the Piedmont, further dissipated Cornwallis' energies at Guilford Courthouse, and prepared the way for the American victory at Yorktown.

By providing an unexpected American victory on the South Carolina border, Kings Mountain prevented the immediate subjugation of the Carolinas and temporarily deranged the British campaign to establish a completely conquered southern base of operation. By producing a feeling of patriotic success at the inception of the final major British campaign, Kings Mountain contributed to the renewing of American resistance which resulted in the British disasters of 1781.

The American Rifle

At the Battle of Kings Mountain[2]

By C. P. Russell, Chief Naturalist
Branch of Natural History

Progress made on the new museum at Kings Mountain National Military Park, South Carolina, is worthy of record, and the fact that the Service possesses a Ferguson rifle to put into that museum constitutes special note within the record. To the average park visitor "Ferguson rifle" means little or nothing, but to the student of military history mention of that British weapon kindles a flame of interest. The story of how the Ferguson rifle was pitted against the Kentucky rifle at Kings Mountain is significant in this day of rearmament.

Maj. Patrick Ferguson was born in 1744, the son of a Scottish jurist, James Ferguson of Pitfour. At an early age he became an officer in the Royal North British Dragoons, and by the time the American colonists revolted against British rule he had distinguished himself in service with the Scotch militia and as an expeditionist during the Carib insurrection in the West Indies. In 1776 he demonstrated to British Government officials a weapon of his own invention, "a rifle gun on a new construction which astonished all beholders."

14

BREECH MECHANISM
OF THE FERGUSON RIFLE

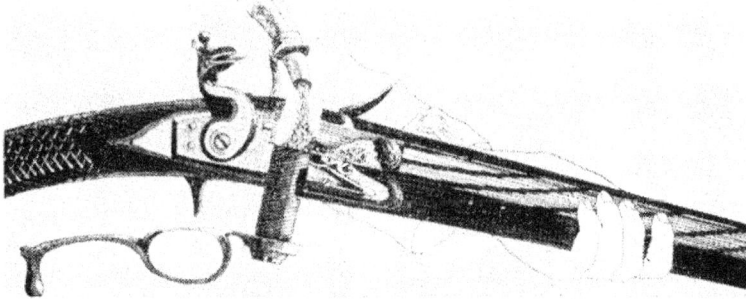

BREECH MECHANISM OF THE FERGUSON RIFLE
Breech plug lowered by one turn of the trigger guard

The remarkable feature of the gun is its perpendicular breech plug equipped with a screw device so as to make it possible to lower it by a revolution of the trigger guard which serves as a handle. When the breech plug is lowered, an opening is left in the top of the barrel at the breech. A spherical bullet dropped into this opening with the muzzle of the gun held downward rolls forward through the chamber where it is stopped by the lands of the rifling. A charge of powder then poured into the opening fills the chamber behind the bullet, whereupon one revolution of the trigger guard closes the breech and the weapon is ready for priming and firing. Major Ferguson demonstrated that six aimed shots per minute could be fired with an accuracy creditable to any rifle. Advancing riflemen could fire four aimed shots per minute; reloading being possible while the marksman was running. Another great advantage of the Ferguson rifle was found in the fact that it could be loaded while the marksman was reclining—something quite impossible with the American rifle. A patent was granted for the Ferguson invention on December 2, 1776, and the weapon became the first breechloader used by organized troops of any country.

On September 11, 1777, Major Ferguson commanded the small unit of picked riflemen of the British Army who covered the advance of Knyphauser and his German mercenaries at Brandywine. An American who knew nothing of breechloading rifles, but who was possessed of the old dependable Kentucky rifle, put a bullet into Ferguson's right arm, shattering the elbow. The major's arm was useless thereafter and while he was recuperating Sir William Howe jealously took advantage of his disability, disbanded Ferguson's riflemen, and put into storage the superior rifles which they had carried. This did not terminate the service of Ferguson, nor did it relegate his rifle to the discard. His command was restored, and he again took the field with his handful of riflemen. At Stony Point, N. Y., and Little Egg Harbor, N. J., he came out on top in the fighting with American privateers and the famous Pulaski Legion. Had Great Britain manufactured more of the Ferguson rifles, perhaps he would have gained further victories.

Sir Henry Clinton's expedition of 1779 against Charleston, S. C., found Ferguson and a comparatively few of his rifles active in the depredations of several thousand Tories organized to terrorize the rebellious colonists of the Carolinas. They invaded the interior and operated on the very western border of the Carolinas. For 5 months he held sway over the upcountry, enticing or intimidating the young men of the region to enlist under the British flag. The local militia so formed in the wild back country were drilled by him in the ways of the British Army, and all other inhabitants, so far as possible, were pledged to faithful Royal service. The patriots of the interior settlements lay helpless. Any Carolinian found in arms against the King might be— and many were—hanged for treason. Finally, a British proclamation was issued requiring all inhabitants to take active part on the royalist side, which but served to bring about a notable uprising of the Whigs who, throughout the summer of 1780, engaged in fierce guerilla warfare against the organized Tories.

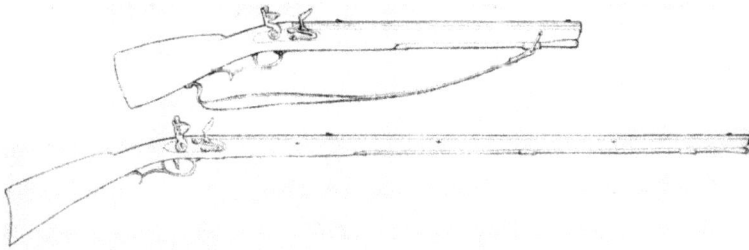

German Jäger rifle, used in America during the Revolution, above; as compared with the Kentucky rifle of the Revolutionary period, below.

Not only did the sparsely populated settlements on the headwaters of the Catawba, Broad, and Pacolet Rivers contribute to the force that opposed Ferguson, but the over-mountain settlements on the Watauga and Holston likewise sent their backwoodsmen, all of whom were well experienced in Indian warfare. The routes followed by these parties on their way to the Kings Mountain rendezvous cross the present Blue Ridge National Parkway in a number of places.

The unmerciful treatment of Buford's patriots at the hands of Tarleton had engendered savage fury on the part of the Whigs which was as bitterly reciprocated by the Tories. Utter refusal of quarter was usual in many battles. In the Carolinas, hand-to-hand encounters were common, and the contest became a war of ruthless extermination. General Greene, writing of this condition, said: "The animosity between the Whigs and Tories renders their situation truly deplorable.... The Whigs seem determined to extirpate the Tories, and the Tories the Whigs.... If a stop cannot be put to these massacres, the country will be depopulated in a few months more, as neither Whig nor Tory can live."

In September 1780, while this spirit of hatred was at its height, the regiments of backwoods patriots, who were to go down in history as "Kings Mountain Men," rendezvoused at South Mountain north of Gilbert Town and determined to set upon Ferguson and his command, then believed to be in Gilbert Town. The followers of the Whig border leaders, Campbell, Shelby, Sevier, Cleveland, Lacey, Williams, McDowell, Hambright, Hawthorne, Brandon, Chronicle, and Hammond, descended upon Gilbert Town on October 4 only to find that the Tories, apprised of the planned attack, had evacuated that place; Ferguson was in full retreat in an attempt to evade an engagement. His goal was Charlotte and the safety of the British forces there stationed under Cornwallis. On October 6, Ferguson was attracted from his line of march to the commanding eminence, Kings Mountain, known at that time by the famous name that we apply today. His 1,100 loyalists went into camp on these heights, and Ferguson declared that "he was on Kings Mountain, that he was King of that mountain, and God Almighty could not drive him from it." He took none of the ordinary military precautions of forming breastworks, but merely placed his baggage wagons along the northeastern part of the mountain to give some slight appearance of protection in the neighborhood of his headquarters.

The united backwoodsmen, led by Campbell, had pursued the fleeing Tories from Gilbert Town. Spies sent forward obtained accurate information on the numbers and intentions of the Tories. It became evident to the Whig leaders that, if they were to overtake their quarry before reinforcements sent by Cornwallis might join them, a more speedy pursuit would be necessary. Accordingly, on the night of October 5, the best men, horses, and equipment were selected for a forced march. About 900 picked horsemen, all well armed with the Kentucky rifle, traveled by way of Cowpens, S. C., marching throughout the rainy night of October 6, crossed the swollen Broad River at Cherokee Ford, and on the afternoon of October 7 came upon the Loyalists on their supposed stronghold.

The story of the battle which ensued is one of the thrilling chapters in our history. The Whigs surrounded the mountain and, in spite of a few bayonet charges made by the Tories, pressed up the slopes and poured into the Loyalist lines such deadly fire from the long rifles that in less than an hour 225 had been killed, 163 wounded, and 716 made prisoners. Major Ferguson fell with eight bullets in his body. The Whigs lost 28 killed and 62 wounded.

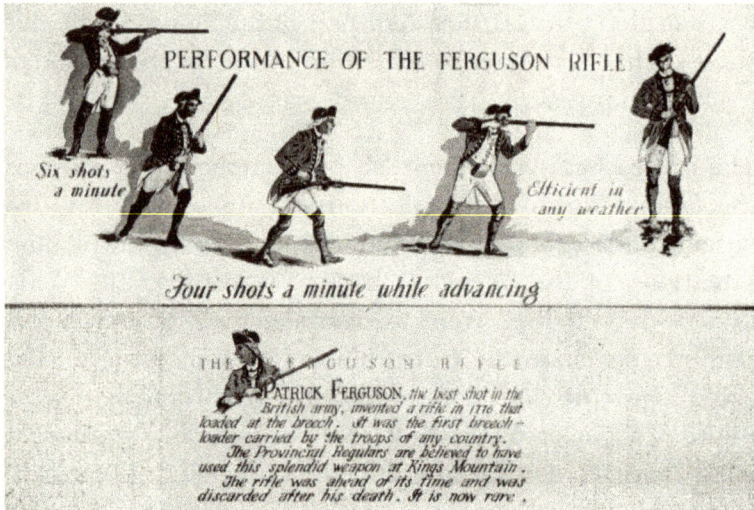

PERFORMANCE OF THE FERGUSON RIFLE
Six shots a minute
Efficient in any weather
Four shots a minute while advancing
THE FERGUSON RIFLE

PATRICK FERGUSON, *the best shot in the British army, invented a rifle in 1776 that loaded at the breech. It was the first breechloader carried by the troops of any country.*

The Provincial Regulars are believed to have used this splendid weapon at Kings Mountain.

The rifle was ahead of its time and was discarded after his death. It is now rare.

Probably no other battle in the Revolution was so picturesque or so furiously fought as that at Kings Mountain. The very mountain thundered. Not a regular soldier was in the American ranks. Every man there was actuated by a spirit of democracy. They fought under leaders of their own choosing for the right to live in a land governed by men of their own choice.

With the death of Ferguson, the rifles of his invention, with which probably 150 of his men were armed, disappeared. Some were broken in the fight and others were carried off by the victors. One given by Ferguson to his companion, De Peyster, is today an heirloom in the family of the latter's descendants in New York City. It was exhibited by the United States Government at the World's Fair at Chicago in 1893. A very few are to be found in museum collections in this country and in England. The one possessed by the National Park Service was obtained from a dealer in England through the vigilance of members of the staff of the Colonial National Historical Park, Virginia, and is now exhibited in the museum at Kings Mountain National Military Park, South Carolina.

The Kings Mountain museum tells the story of the Revolutionary backwoodsman and his place in the scheme of Americanism. Here also is presented the story of the cultural, social, and economic background of the Kings Mountain patriots, as well as the details of the battle and its effect on the Revolution as a whole. Here lies the rare opportunity to preserve for all time significant relics of Colonial and Revolutionary days and at the same time interpret for a multitude of visitors the basic elements in the story of the old frontier—a story which affected most of the Nation during the century that followed the Revolution.

Our interest here will turn to those intriguing reminders of how our Colonial ancestors lived—their houses, their tools and implements, their furniture, their books, and their guns. Because of the significance of the American rifle in the battle of Kings Mountain, it must be a feature of any Kings Mountain exhibit. In the Carolinas it was as much a part of each patriot as was his good right arm.

Light in weight, graceful in line, economical in consumption of powder and lead, fatally precise, and distinctly American, it was for 100 years the great arbitrator that settled all differences throughout the American wilderness. George Washington, while a surveyor in the back country, as scout and diplomat on his march into the Ohio country, and while with his Virginians on Braddock's fatal expedition, had formed the acquaintance of the hunters, Indian fighters, and pioneers of the Alleghanies — riflemen all. These men were drawn upon in 1775 to form the first units of the United States Army, 10 companies of "expert riflemen." The British, in an attempt to compete with American accuracy of fire, cried for Jäger, German huntsmen armed with rifles, and begged that they might be included in the contingents of German troops.

From the numerous written comments on the American rifle and riflemen made by British leaders, it would be possible to quote at length regarding the effect of American rifle fire upon British morale and casualty lists. We may call attention again to the statistics on the Kings Mountain dead: British, 225; American, 28. Draper records that 20 dead Tories were found behind certain protruding rocks on the crest of the hill, and that each victim was marked by a bullet hole in his forehead. Col. George Hanger, British officer with Tarleton in South Carolina, provides the following observation on the precision of American rifle fire:

> I never in my life saw better rifles (or men who shot better) than those made in America; they are chiefly made in Lancaster, and two or three neighboring towns in that vicinity, in Pennsylvania. The barrels weigh about six pounds two or three ounces, and carry a ball no larger than thirty-six to the pound; at least I never saw one of the larger caliber, and I have seen many hundreds and

hundreds. I am not going to relate any thing respecting the American war; but to mention one instance, as a proof of most excellent skill of an American rifleman. If any man shew me an instance of better shooting, I will stand corrected.

Colonel, now General Tartleton, and myself, were standing a few yards out of a wood, observing the situation of a part of the enemy which we intended to attack. There was a rivulet in the enemy's front, and a mill on it, to which we stood directly with our horses' heads fronting, observing their motions. It was an absolute plain field between us and the mill; not so much as a single bush on it. Our orderly-bugle stood behind us, about 3 yards, but with his horse's side to our horses' tails. A rifleman passed over the mill-dam, evidently observing two officers, and laid himself down on his belly; for, in such positions, they always lie, to take a good shot at a long distance. He took a deliberate and cool shot at my friend, at me, and the bugle-horn man. (I have passed several times over this ground, and ever observed it with the greatest attention; and I can positively assert that the distance he fired from, at us, was full four hundred yards.)

Now, observe how well this fellow shot. It was in the month of August, and not a breath of wind was stirring. Colonel Tartleton's horse and mine, I am certain, were not anything like two feet apart; for we were in close consultation, how we should attack with our troops, which laid 300 yards in the wood, and could not be perceived by the enemy. A rifle-ball passed between him and me; looking directly to the mill, I observed the flash of the powder. I said to my friend, "I think we had better move, or we shall have two or three of these gentlemen, shortly, amusing themselves at our expence." The words were hardly out of my mouth, when the bugle horn man, behind us, and directly central, jumped off his horse, and said, "Sir, my horse is shot." The horse staggered, fell down, and died. He was shot directly behind the foreleg, near to the heart, at least where the great blood-vessels lie, which lead to the heart. He took the saddle and bridle off, went into the woods, and got another horse. We had a number of spare horses, led by negro lads.

The rifle had been introduced into America about 1700 when there was considerable immigration into Pennsylvania from Switzerland and Austria, the only part of the world at that time where it was in use. It was then short, heavy, clumsy, and little more accurate than the musket. From this arm the American gunsmiths evolved the long, slender, small-bore gun (about 36 balls to the pound) which by 1750 had reached the same state of development that characterized it at the time of the Revolution. The German Jäger rifle brought to America during the Revolution was by no means the equal of the American piece. It was short-barreled and took a ball of 19 to the pound. With its large ball and small powder charge its recoil was heavy and its accurate range but little greater than that of the smoothbore musket. It was the same gun that had been introduced into America in 1700.

The standard military firearm of the Revolutionary period was the flintrock musket weighing about 11 pounds. Its caliber was 11 gauge, that is, it would take a lead ball of 11 to the pound. At 100 yards a good marksman might make 40 percent of hits on a target the size of a man standing. The musket ball, fitting loosely in the barrel, could be loaded quickly. The fact that the military musket always was equipped with a bayonet made it the dependable weapon for all close fighting. As was so convincingly shown on the occasions of the futile bayonet charges of Ferguson's regulars on Kings Mountain, however, the bayonet was not effective if enemy lines did not stand to take the punishment of hand-to-hand fighting.

Each Whig on Kings Mountain had been told to act as his own captain, to yield as he found it necessary, and to take every advantage that was presented. In short, the patriots followed the Indian mode of attack, using the splendid cover that the timber about the mountain afforded, and selecting a definite human target for every ball fired. Splendid leadership and command were exercised by the Whig officers to make for concerted action every time a crisis arose. This coordination, plus the Kentucky rifle and the "individual power of woodcraft, marksmanship, and sportsmanship" of each participant in the American forces, overcame all the military training and discipline which had been injected into his Tory troops by Ferguson.

Testing the Ferguson Rifle

Modern Marksman Attains High Precision With Arm of 1776[3]

By Dr. Alfred F. Hopkins, formerly Field Curator, Museum Division, Washington.

History records that on June 1, 1776, at Woolwich, England, Maj. Patrick Ferguson, of the British Army, demonstrated his newly devised breechloading flintrock rifle to the astonishment of all beholders. Quite recently at the Washington laboratory of the Museum Division of the National Park Service beholders likewise were astonished at the shooting qualities of the Ferguson gun.

While it is understood that tests of this historic arm have been made in England within late years, it is believed that in this country the sinister crack of a Ferguson had not been heard since 1780 at the Battle of Kings Mountain, South Carolina.

Ferguson developed his rifle from two earlier types of breechloaders, the Hardley and the Foster, upon which it was an actual improvement, and his gun has the distinction of being the first breechloading arm used by organized troops of any nation. The piece is equipped with a breechplug which passes perpendicularly through the breech of the barrel and this, having a quick-traveling screw thread, is lowered or raised by a single revolution of the trigger guard acting as a lever. When the breech plug is lowered, a circular opening is left in the top of the barrel just large enough to take a spherical bullet. In loading, the muzzle is held downward and the ball, fitting snugly, is

26

dropped into the opening and permitted to roll forward to the front of the breech chamber where it is stopped by the lands of the rifling. No wadding or patch is used. Powder and ball rolled to form a cartridge would prove only a hindrance and disadvantage in loading. A charge of powder is poured directly from a flask or horn into the opening behind the bullet, filling the chamber. One complete turn of the trigger guard causes the breech plug to rise, closing the opening and ejecting the superfluous grains of powder. When the flashpan is primed, the piece is ready for firing. In the third illustration of this booklet the breech mechanism and method of loading are shown. Major Ferguson is accredited with loading and firing six shots in one minute.

No recent check is known to have been made upon the number of Ferguson rifles now in existence. They undoubtedly do exist, but their number is probably small. Apparently only some 200 were made originally and their military use ended, owing to lack of foresight, with the American Revolution. Six specimens were listed in 1928 as being in collections in this country and in England, of which one, probably two, were made by Newton, of Grantham, two by Egg, of London, and one each by Turner and Wilson, of London. These six guns varied somewhat in minor details.

A seventh specimen, the one now possessed by the Service at Kings Mountain National Military Park, South Carolina, bears the name of F. Innis, Edinburgh. It is in exceptionally fine condition, showing much of the original metal finish, and is without replacements. The piece measures 4 feet 4¾ inches over all and weighs 7½ pounds. The barrel, slightly belled at the muzzle and not designed to carry a bayonet, is 37 inches long, rifled with 8 grooves, and takes a ball of .655 caliber. The full length combed walnut stock is checkered at the grip and has three brass thimbles and an engraved butt plate. On the lock plate forward the hammer, within a scroll, is the name, F. INNIS, and this, with the addition of EDINBURGH, together with the proof mark and the view mark of the Gunmakers' Company of London, appears upon the barrel. The wooden ramrod is horn-tipped and at the other end has a bullet worm enclosed within a screw cap. The arm was intended for an officer.

The Centennial Monument at Kings Mountain, unveiled on the 100th anniversary of the Battle, October 7, 1880.

The recent tests conducted indoors at the Ford's Theater Laboratory were made to determine the exact method of loading the arm, about which there had been some question, and to learn something of its shooting qualities. Loading was found to be extremely easy, suggesting that with practice the record set by Major Ferguson might be attained readily. The ball, weighing approximately 500 grains, was dropped, without patch or wad, into the breech chamber. A charge of approximately 1½ drams of Dupont "Fg" black powder was poured in behind it. Closure of the breech automatically gauged the charge, superfluous grains being ejected. The same powder, more finely ground, was used as priming. Several preliminary shots indicated that the rifle had precision and accuracy. Then, at a distance of 90 feet, three shots were fired in succession from a table rest by an expert marksman. Number one came within a half-inch, number two came within 4 inches, and number three came within 1¾ inches of a 1⅝-inch bull's-eye.

View of the Kings Mountain region, taken from the eastern slope of the battlefield ridge, looking northeastwardly toward Henry's Knob.

Granite obelisk erected by the Federal Government at Kings Mountain in 1909 to commemorate the Battle.

U. S. GOVERNMENT PRINTING OFFICE: 1947

Footnotes

[1] From *The Regional Review*, National Park Service, Region One, Richmond, Va., Vol. III, No. 6, December 1939, pp. 25-29.

[2] From *Idem.*, vol. V, No. 1, July 1940, pp. 15-21.

[3] *Idem.*, vol. VI, Nos. 1 and 2.

National Park Service
Popular Study Series

No. 1.—Winter Encampments of the Revolution.

No. 2.—Weapons and Equipment of Early American Soldiers.

No. 3.—Wall Paper News of the Sixties.

No. 4.—Prehistoric Cultures in the Southeast.

No. 5.—Mountain Speech in the Great Smokies.

No. 6.—New Echota, Birthplace of the American Indian Press.

No. 7.—Hot Shot Furnaces.

No. 8.—Perry at Put in Bay: Echoes of the War of 1812.

No. 9.—Wharf Building of a Century and More Ago.

No. 10.—Gardens of the Colonists.

No. 11.—Robert E. Lee and Fort Pulaski.

No. 12.—Rifles and Riflemen at the Battle of Kings Mountain.

No. 13.—Rifle Making in the Great Smoky Mountains.

No. 14.—American Charcoal Making in the Era of the Cold Blast Furnace.